The Gospel on the Move

The Gospel on the Move

How the Cross Transcends Cultural Differences

A Reflection by Timothy Keller

GOSPEL IN LIFE

The Gospel on the Move

Copyright © 2024 by Timothy Keller

Published 2024 by Gospel in Life

ISBN: 978-1-944549-11-4

This reflection is based off of Timothy Keller's sermon "The Gospel to the Ethiopian," which was preached in 2013 at Redeemer Presbyterian Church in New York City.

For more resources from Timothy Keller, visit GospelinLife.com

All rights reserved. No part of this publication may be reproduced, distributed, or transmitted in any form or by any means, including photocopying, recording, or other electronic or mechanical methods, without the prior written permission of the publisher, except in the case of brief quotations embodied in critical reviews and certain other noncommercial uses permitted by copyright law.

Scripture taken from The Holy Bible, New International Version®, NIV® Copyright © 1973, 1978, 1984, 2011 by Biblica, Inc.® Used by permission. All rights reserved worldwide.

Editors: Kathy Keller, Braeden Gregg, Linda Ann

Cover and Interior Design: Lee Marcum

Printed in the United States of America

TABLE OF CONTENTS

Foreword by Kathy Keller — v

ONE Scripture — 1

TWO Introduction — 5

THREE The Inclusivity of Christianity — 9

FOUR The Exclusivity of Christianity — 21

FIVE The Reason for Both — 27

SIX A Prayer for God's Guidance — 39

Endnotes — 43

About — 47

FOREWARD
BY KATHY KELLER

FOREWORD

This was a sermon that Tim particularly loved. At one time he preached a version of it to the national Young Life leaders' conference. The line I remember had to do with "contact work," which is what YL leaders are told to do in order to get to know their high school students—just hang out with them. "You think contact work is hard, do you? Well, think of Philip jogging along, trying to keep up with that chariot and carry on a conversation. 'Hey, whatcha reading? Understand it much?'"

It got a big laugh, but Tim wasn't wrong. That's exactly what Philip was doing . . . jogging next to a chariot, carrying on a conversation about the Bible. How did that happen?

Acts 8:5 tells us that "Philip went down to a city in Samaria and proclaimed the Messiah there." What was Philip doing preaching the gospel in Samaria? A few verses earlier in chapter 8, we are told that on the day Stephen was stoned to death, a "great persecution broke out against the church in Jerusalem, and all except the apostles were scattered throughout Judea and Samaria . . . [and] those who had been scattered preached the word wherever they went" (Acts 8:1, 4).

This should not be a surprise, because Jesus had warned his disciples that they would be persecuted in all manner of ways, including death, because "If the world hates you, keep in mind that it hated me first. If you belonged to the world, it would love you as its own. As it is, you do not belong to the world, but I have chosen you out of the world. That is why the world hates you. Remember what I told you: 'A servant is not greater than his master.' If they persecuted me, they will persecute you also" (John 15:18-20).

However, if we think a little harder, we should wonder why all the Christians had been congregating in Jerusalem to begin with.

MATTHEW 28:18-20

Jesus had given his followers what is known as the Great Commission: "Therefore go and make disciples of all nations, baptizing them in the name of the Father and of the Son and of the Holy Spirit."

ACTS 1:8

And he had reinforced this at his ascension when he told them: "You will receive power when the Holy Spirit comes on you; and you will be my witnesses in Jerusalem, and in all Judea and Samaria, and to the ends of the earth."

But for a long while, nothing happened. No one went rushing to pack for a trip to Samaria and parts beyond.

The disciples and the first converts remained in Jerusalem, growing in number and maturity, but continuing to worship at the temple. They were universally known as a "Jewish sect," and they had no pressing motivation to move from the familiarity of Jerusalem and the Jewish world they had always known into "the ends of the earth" to "make disciples of all nations."

When Stephen was stoned to death, a widespread persecution of Christians began, both by Jewish opponents, who considered them heretics, as well as by Roman authorities who viewed their refusal to worship Roman gods as civil disobedience and an insult to the Emperor.

So let's first take note that God often uses painful means to move us to accomplish his will for us. Persecution and suffering should move Christians into high gear for sharing the gospel. And in the New Testament it did. I have to say that I grieve that what many North American Christians regard as persecution a) doesn't even come close to what the early disciples experienced or to what present-day Christians in other parts of the world are currently experiencing, and b) has not resulted in a revival of evangelism, holiness, concern for others, or other fruit of the Spirit.

So having set the stage, Philip is in Samaria (a place, as far as we can tell, where no Christians had ever wanted to go to before), and he's preaching the word of the Lord and seeing that the Holy Spirit fell on them just as it had on the Jewish believers. That must have been paradigm shifting!! After God gave a direct miracle showing that he had really meant what Jesus had said about making disciples in Samaria, an angel then directed Philip to another encounter that showed what God thought of human barriers and divisions. Philip was sent to walk on a road from Jerusalem to Gaza. No further instructions, just "Go south and walk." When he got to the road, the Spirit gave him further (but not very complete) instructions: "Go to that chariot and stay near it."

To understand what happens next you have to read the rest of this booklet. I hope it will encourage you to obey God in persecution. I hope you will obey God when his instructions *seem* partial, incomplete, or even puzzling, and that you obey God so that you will see lives changed—both yours and the lives of people who may be very different from you.

In praise for a sovereign God,
Kathy Keller

CHAPTER

SCRIPTURE

SCRIPTURE

ACTS 8:26–40

[26] Now an angel of the Lord said to Philip, "Go south to the road—the desert road—that goes down from Jerusalem to Gaza." [27] So he started out, and on his way he met an Ethiopian eunuch, an important official in charge of all the treasury of the Kandake (which means "queen of the Ethiopians"). This man had gone to Jerusalem to worship, [28] and on his way home was sitting in his chariot reading the Book of Isaiah the prophet. [29] The Spirit told Philip, "Go to that chariot and stay near it."

[30] Then Philip ran up to the chariot and heard the man reading Isaiah the prophet. "Do you understand what you are reading?" Philip asked.

[31] "How can I," he said, "unless someone explains it to me?" So he invited Philip to come up and sit with him.

[32] This is the passage of Scripture the eunuch was reading:

"He was led like a sheep to the slaughter,
   and as a lamb before its shearer is silent,
   so he did not open his mouth.
[33] In his humiliation he was deprived of justice.
   Who can speak of his descendants?
   For his life was taken from the earth."

³⁴ The eunuch asked Philip, "Tell me, please, who is the prophet talking about, himself or someone else?" ³⁵ Then Philip began with that very passage of Scripture and told him the good news about Jesus.

³⁶ As they traveled along the road, they came to some water and the eunuch said, "Look, here is water. What can stand in the way of my being baptized?" [³⁷] ³⁸ And he gave orders to stop the chariot. Then both Philip and the eunuch went down into the water and Philip baptized him. ³⁹ When they came up out of the water, the Spirit of the Lord suddenly took Philip away, and the eunuch did not see him again, but went on his way rejoicing. ⁴⁰ Philip, however, appeared at Azotus and traveled about, preaching the gospel in all the towns until he reached Caesarea.

CHAPTER

INTRODUCTION

INTRODUCTION

The book of Acts records the earliest beginnings of Christianity following Christ's return to heaven. It teaches us about the character of the earliest Christians and how the power of God overturned the world. And the more I consider this story of Philip and the Ethiopian, the more I regard it with amazement.

This passage brings to mind a single line in a poem by George Herbert, a seventeenth-century poet. It goes like this: "Bibles laid open, millions of surprises...."[1] No matter who you are, the Bible will surprise you. No matter what your culture or class is, no matter what preconceptions you bring to the Bible, it will confront them.

This is a surprising, category-shattering text. I'd like to look at it through three different principles it teaches us. For starters, it tells us about the inclusivity of Christianity. Secondly, it tells us about the exclusivity of Christianity. Finally, we learn the reasoning and grounding for both. Most people say, "Well, you're either inclusive or exclusive," but the fact is that Christianity is radically inclusive and radically exclusive. It *can* be both because it *is* both.

CHAPTER

3

THE INCLUSIVITY OF
CHRISTIANITY

THE INCLUSIVITY OF CHRISTIANITY

We're told the main figure in the story is an Ethiopian eunuch. At that time, Ethiopia referred to the Upper Nile region of Africa from as far north as Aswan and as far south as Khartoum. Today, we call it Nubia.

Furthermore, he was a eunuch. He had been castrated. For people in his position, that was common. If you weren't part of the royal family, but you were being groomed for administrative leadership in government and were in close proximity with royal family members, the price was castration. It removed temptation on the part of the administrator and suspicion on the part of the royal family, but at a terrible cost.

Right away, we notice two things. First, how different the two people are in this story. Philip was a middle-class Jewish man. The man in the chariot was Black. He was from the outermost part of the known civilized world. He was sexually altered. From the view of Philip's culture, this man would have been considered a racially different, sexually altered barbarian—as different from Philip as possible.

In those days, Jewish men got up every day and prayed, "O Lord, I thank you that you didn't make me a woman, a slave, or a Gentile." They were told, "You don't want to associate with people who are different from you, because it defiles you." Yet the Ethiopian was about as different from Philip as a person could be.

The second thing to notice is how direct God's intervention had to be in order for this connection to be made. In verse 26, an angel of the Lord told Philip to go to the road that goes down from Jerusalem to Gaza. Secondly, verse 29 says that when he sees the Ethiopian, "The Spirit told Philip, 'Go to that chariot and stay near it.' Then Philip ran up to the chariot."

Do you know why the Spirit had to say, "Go to the chariot and stay near it"? Because it was moving. He had to run! He wasn't invited into the chariot until verse 31, so who knows how long he had to jog along before he was noticed. Up until then, he must have been running alongside, waiting to see what God had in mind. He saw the Ethiopian was reading Scripture and asked, "Do you understand what you're reading?" This was not the usual way chance encounters on the road unfolded. Then the eunuch invited Philip to come up and sit with him. (Have you ever wondered why he would do that? He picked up a guy who wasn't even hitchhiking!) Once he was inside, Philip immediately seized on a commonality that unites men who are seemingly very different: the Bible.

Bear in mind that this meeting never would have happened unless the Spirit had said to go and run alongside. And we're told at the very end, in verse 39, that as soon as the baptism happened, the Spirit took

Philip. We don't know quite how he did it, but it's a word that literally means "seize." The Spirit seized Philip and took him away. By every measure, this was a divine encounter. Every single aspect of it happened because of divine intervention.

We can learn two important things from the way this was set up. First of all, the Spirit of God strongly desires for racial barriers between people to be surmounted. It's one of the most obvious themes throughout the book of Acts. Over and over again, the Spirit stirs Christians to break barriers, get out of their comfort zone, and embrace people of different races, cultures, and locations.

The Bible talks about the Spirit being grieved if we don't love what God loves. This must mean it grieves God when Christians of one race show disdain for or ignore people of other races, temperaments, classes, and cultures. It grieves the Spirit. Friends, we must listen to the voice of the Spirit. Here it is: Philip, run up to that racially different, physically altered man you would ordinarily have nothing to do with . . . and stay close. That's the trajectory of the Spirit in the whole book of Acts, and it's still the trajectory of the Spirit. The Spirit of God desires that racial, economic, and personal barriers be surmounted. And it begins by making the effort (you think it was easy keeping up with a horse-drawn chariot?) to stay close. To begin with, don't talk, don't push yourself on anyone—wait to be invited in and just stay close.

Secondly, the other thing we learn here is that Christianity does not belong to one culture more than another. Over and over in the book of Acts, we see non-Jews getting converted. First, Samaritans were converted. Though they were geographically close, Samaritans were racially alienated by the Jews because the two groups hated each other.

Now a Black African gets converted, someone who's not just racially different but also geographically from the far reaches of the then-known world. Later in the book, we see a Jewish Pharisee getting converted by the gospel. Then, Romans get converted by the gospel. Over and over again, the book of Acts fails to favor one culture as the one to which Christianity belongs more to than another.

During Jesus's ascension into Heaven, Luke 24 states that he gave his followers this command:

> 46 He told them, "This is what is written: The Messiah will suffer and rise from the dead on the third day, 47 and repentance for the forgiveness of sins will be preached in his name to all nations, beginning at Jerusalem."

THE INCLUSIVITY OF CHRISTIANITY

Matthew records the same occasion in chapter 28, saying:

> [18] Then Jesus came to them and said, "All authority in heaven and on earth has been given to me. [19] Therefore go and make disciples of all nations, baptizing them in the name of the Father and of the Son and of the Holy Spirit, [20] and teaching them to obey everything I have commanded you."

Do you know how that puts the Bible into direct conflict with the ordinary understanding of how culture and religion relate? Today, most colleges or schools will teach that religion is just an extension or a function of culture. It's not unusual for students to hear something along the lines of this: "Religion is an invention of culture because every culture needs solidarity. In every culture, people need cohesiveness based on shared customs and values to keep that culture together. One of the ways to do that is to spin out these metaphysical, spiritual stories that become religion. So, Europeans and North Americans developed Christianity, South Asian cultures developed Hinduism, Far Eastern cultures developed Buddhism, Confucianism, and Shintoism, and the Middle Eastern, North African, and some South Asian cultures developed Islam. Every culture develops a religion as an extension of itself, and that's all religion is."

Lamin Sanneh, an African professor at Yale (and a Christian), wrote a terrific little book some years ago called *Whose Religion Is Christianity? The Gospel Beyond the West*. He points out that if you look at where the population centers are for the major world religions, their population centers are still roughly near where they started—except for Christianity.[1]

The majority of other religions' adherents are still located in the cultures where those religions were developed. For example, 88% percent of Buddhists live in East Asia and 95% percent of Hindus live in India or South Asia.[2] This does, of course, play into the theory that religion is just an extension of culture.

But Sanneh points out that Christianity is absolutely different. It's the only worldwide religion: 25% of Christians are in Europe, 25% are in Latin America and the Caribbean, 22% are in Africa, and 15% are in Asia, but that number is growing very fast. Only 12% of all of the Christians in the world are in North America.[2]

Korea went from 0% of a Christian population to having about 40 or 50% of one in about 100 years. China—which is quite a bit bigger than Korea, by the way—is doing the same thing right now over a 100-year period (thus the reason I said the percentage of

Christians in Asia is growing very rapidly). Africa went from being about 9% Christian to 44% Christian in 100 years.[3]

No other religion has ever spread across the continents like Christianity has. It's just never happened before. In fact, Richard Bauckham, former scholar at the University of St. Andrews in Scotland, says, "Almost certainly, Christianity exhibits more cultural diversity than any other religion, and that must say something about it."[4] Absolutely it says something about it. Why is it that Christianity is far more inclusive of cultural diversity than any other religion and, therefore, really the only worldwide and culturally diverse religion?

Sanneh gives an example from the African perspective. He tells us to consider this: Africans have always believed the world was a supernatural place. They've always believed the world was filled with spirits, both good and evil. That's at the heart of what it means to be an African. But what is one to do about the evil spirits? They're powerful. They can seduce you over to evil and dominate you. How does someone avoid this?

Many environments that espouse inclusivity still find themselves ill-equipped to answer cultural concerns like these. For example, Sanneh says if an African goes off to a secular country or a secular school such as Oxford, Yale, Princeton, or the like, these places will usually tell them, "Oh, we're very inclusive. We're multicultural. We're very happy for you to eat your African food and wear your African dress." But out of the same mouth, they will also tell them there are no spirits. "There are no demons, no angels, none of that stuff. Everything has a scientific explanation." In other words, Sanneh states, they say, "We really love your culture; we're just going to take the heart out of it. You still have to become a late-modern, secular, individualistic Westerner like us or you're not enlightened." That's not inclusive! That's exploitative.

But, as Sanneh also says, when Christianity comes to Africa, it goes like this: Christianity challenges and yet accepts "Africanness." It says, "On one hand, you're right: the world is a supernatural place. There are a lot of good spirits and evil spirits. But there is One who has overcome the evil spirits: Jesus Christ. And through him, you can overcome them too." Sanneh says that affirms Africanness and yet renews it:

> [Africans] sensed in their hearts that Jesus did not mock their respect for the sacred or their clamor for an invincible Savior, and so they beat their sacred drums for him until the stars skipped and danced in the skies. After that dance the stars weren't little anymore. Christianity

helped Africans to become renewed Africans, not re-made Europeans.[5]

In other words, Christianity is far more inclusive than secularism, which always talks about inclusiveness. Christianity does not just belong to this culture or that culture. It's not an extension, function, or product of culture. It comes down from above. It stands over all culture, and it's the job of the Holy Spirit to recreate Christianity in the soil of every culture. Christianity is, therefore, the most inclusive of all religions—even more inclusive than secularism.

CHAPTER

THE EXCLUSIVITY OF
CHRISTIANITY

THE EXCLUSIVITY OF CHRISTIANITY

This point is shorter, and I'll tell you why. If you live in an environment that values inclusivity, you're probably getting this good feeling from all this talk of inclusion. Just hearing the word "inclusive" is enough to make the average Manhattanite feel warm and fuzzy inside. To actually see empirical evidence that Christianity is the religion most inclusive of cultural differences just has a nice feel to it, doesn't it?

But if you want to understand why Christianity is more culturally inclusive than secularism or than other religions, you need to see how it's exclusive. The reason this is a short point is that it probably doesn't take as many arguments to make the case that Christianity makes exclusive claims. You can see them right here.

For example, the Ethiopian eunuch was reading the scroll of Isaiah when he asked Philip, in verse 34, what this text means. Obviously, Philip did not respond in a postmodern, literary, theoretical way. He didn't say, "You have to create the meaning of the text for yourself. You have to decide what is right or wrong for you. I can't tell you." He told him that Jesus is the hermeneutical and interpretative principle that makes sense of everything in the Bible. He told him the gospel. Then the eunuch asked, "Why shouldn't I be baptized?" By asking to be baptized, the man proclaimed his conversion and his faith in Jesus, and his intention to identify with the people of God.

Baptism means one way of life is over and a new way of life begins. Baptism means I stop believing *that* and I start believing *this*. I stop living *that* way; I start living *this* way. He has converted. He wasn't told, "Well, you have to serve God and find God in whatever way is most meaningful for you."

So while you can make a case that Christianity is the most culturally inclusive religion out there, you can also say it's the most exclusive religion. If it's more inclusive than other religions, it's more exclusive as well. How's that? Well, every other religion has a founder who is basically a prophet or a sage or a wise teacher saying, "Here's how to get to God." The image often invoked is that every religion is a different path up to the top of the mountain, but we're all going to the same God. Buddhists say the way to God is to follow the Eightfold Path, and Muslims say the way to God is to practice the Five Pillars. They might seem to teach different practices, but allegedly they're all going to arrive at God at the top of the mountain, each through their own effort and adherence to various teachings. They're different paths to the top, but everyone has to hike to the top by their own effort.

THE EXCLUSIVITY OF CHRISTIANITY

Except Christianity. As we often say, Jesus Christ does not say, "I'm here to show you how to find God." Jesus Christ says, "I am God, and I've come to find you. You'd never get to the top of the mountain by yourself. I've come because I Am the God you're seeking." If that is true, then Christianity is either better than the rest of the world's religions or it's worse, because then Jesus would have told the world's biggest lie. It either has to be better than the rest or worse than the rest. It can't be anything else. Isn't this ironic? Isn't this paradoxical? It means Christianity is the most worldwide, the most culturally diverse, the most inclusive culturally, yet the most exclusive in its claims. How does that work?

CHAPTER

5

THE REASON FOR BOTH

THE REASON FOR BOTH

Understanding this supposed paradox comes down to understanding this story, and the way you get into the heart of the story is asking a question. One of the best ways to understand a story is to ask it the right question, and then let it answer. The question we'll ask is this: Why is the Ethiopian reading the scroll of Isaiah so intently?

This man had gone all the way from his kingdom to Jerusalem to worship at the temple. Why in the world would he do that? First of all, let's think about who he was. He was head of the queen's treasury—he had virtually reached the top. In today's terms, he was the CFO of his country. In fact, he had more power than the United States' Secretary of the Treasury has today. He had power and success, but let's remember that he made a huge sacrifice by becoming a eunuch, and this was in a time when one's descendants were of critical importance. The ancient cultures were not as individualistic as we are today. Today, most people measure their self-worth mainly by their own achievements, but back then, self-worth came from the standing of your family. You only had honor and pride if your family's standing was good. You had no way of having any kind of legacy unless you had children; your sons and daughters were your legacy. Yet here was a man who sacrificed all of that in order to get power. He had given up the very idea of having a family in a completely family-dominated culture. Among other things, that meant loneliness.

So, why would a man take a thousand-mile journey to leave his culture, its religion, and his post? This was a position, by the way, that could have been jeopardized by taking a thousand-mile, year-long trip. The possibility of someone usurping your place would have been pretty good—not to mention how dangerous such a lengthy journey could be.

The answer is there must have been an enormous emptiness in him. His own religion couldn't fill it. All of his power and success couldn't fill it. Why else would he get interested in the God of the Bible, wonder if there was something for him in Jerusalem, and go all the way to the temple? Here's one thing we know: when he got to the temple—after all that travel, all that sacrifice—they wouldn't have let him in.

The temple and all of its worship was regulated by Mosaic Law. The Mosaic law, which is still a little bit of a puzzle to modern readers, had all of these rules about who could get into the temple and worship God and who could not. For example, if you touched a dead body, you were excluded from the temple for a certain amount of time. If you had mold in your house, you were excluded. Why? All of these rules were put into place to get a spiritual idea across. It was often missed, but the idea was that God is holy and we are sinful and shouldn't just walk right into God's dwelling place without being cleansed. Something needed to be done about sin. All of those rules and regulations were like visual aids to try to get that across.

But some of the rules permanently excluded people. One of the rules was that those who had been castrated could never go in and worship God. By that logic, the Ethiopian likely went to all this trouble just to find himself excluded and left outside. You can imagine the disappointment! So, why does he still decide to pore over the book of Isaiah on his way home?

Perhaps a clue lies in which part of the Bible the Ethiopian was reading. The text quoted in the passage is from Isaiah 53, so he was reading the chapters in the 40s and 50s called the "Servant Songs." In chapter 56, which isn't very far from where he was reading, he would have seen this: "Let no foreigner . . . say, 'The Lord will surely exclude me from his people.' And let no eunuch complain, 'I am only a dry tree.' For this is what the Lord says: 'To the eunuchs who . . . hold fast to my covenant, to them I will give . . . a name better than sons and daughters, . . . an everlasting name that will endure forever.'"

Can you imagine his reaction? He would have sat there saying, "Wait a minute. I don't know of any way to pass on my name except through sons and daughters. What is this everlasting name that will never be cut off?"

He's being told in his own cultural terms that there is a salvation that goes beyond not only power and success, but also family. As he's reading, he suddenly realizes there is this strange and enigmatic figure called "the servant" all throughout this part of the Scripture (hence why it's referred to as the "Servant Songs"). God keeps calling someone, "My servant." And this person is suffering. Do you realize why a eunuch would be looking at this passage?

Let's take another look at the specific verse he was reading: "He was led like a sheep to the slaughter, and as a lamb before its shearer is silent, so he did not open his mouth. In his humiliation he was deprived of justice. Who can speak of his descendants? For his life was taken from the earth." Did you notice the part about descendants? In these verses, someone is voluntarily ending their family line, much like a eunuch does, and becoming a lamb to be slain. In fact, if you go a little farther, Isaiah 53:8 says, "By oppression and judgment he was taken away. And who can speak of his descendants? For he was cut off from the land of the living; for the transgression of my people he was punished."[1]

As the Ethiopian sat there wondering who on earth this person was, Philip came up and offered to help him understand what he was reading. He turned to him right away and asked, "Is the prophet talking about himself or someone else?" Philip told him that yes, the prophet was talking about someone very, very, very else—someone absolutely unique. It's Jesus Christ, born in a manger, who died on the cross.

I can imagine Philip telling his new friend something like this: "Jesus became the lamb who was slain. Jesus became like a leper for the lepers. He became like a eunuch for the eunuch. In other words, Jesus Christ was excluded. Don't you see, O my new friend, the Mosaic law was just pointing to a spiritual truth? We're all like eunuchs. We're all excluded from the presence of God. Because of our sins, nobody loves God with all their heart, soul, strength, and mind. Nobody loves their neighbor as themselves. Nobody can go in. We all deserve to be excluded and to be lost. But Jesus Christ was excluded on the cross in place of us. He said, 'My God, my God, why have you forsaken me?' He experienced the God-forsakenness that we deserve. He was excluded so we could be brought in. He was made unclean so we could be cleansed. We could never, ever cleanse ourselves and be good enough on our own, but Jesus Christ has done it for us." That's the good news of Jesus.

Now here's a question: Why is the most inclusive religion the most exclusive, and why would the exclusivity of Christianity bring about this inclusiveness?

First, let's look at what Christianity does. Do you understand why Christianity would be more culturally flexible? What if salvation was like this: God came down as a general and said, "Anyone who obeys everything I tell them will be blessed and successful"? Salvation would be from a strong God to strong people. "Summon up your strength, and be as obedient as you possibly can be."

If salvation were only given to the strong by the strong, Christianity would be a religion of nothing but laws. You would want to be completely compliant because you're only blessed and successful if you're absolutely obedient. Christianity would even tell you what to eat and how to dress and everything. For you to become a Christian, you would have to completely leave behind your culture.

That's not the salvation of the gospel. What is that salvation? The deepest revelation of the nature of God is on the cross. God's greatest glory is seen in how he was willing to lose all of his glory. His greatest beauty is that he was willing to lose his beauty. He became weak, he died and rose again, to take our punishment and the divine wrath. It was the only way to forgive us, the only way to save us, and the only way to someday end evil without ending us. Therefore, the idea of weakness is central to the heart of Christianity.

That means Christianity is not a relativistic religion. There is a universal standard of morality that all cultures must follow. But Christianity also isn't just a religion of truth; it's a religion of truth spoken in love. Even though there are norms, there's a tremendous amount of freedom. There's a softness and a hardness about Christianity. Therefore, it makes perfect sense that Christianity is so flexible, because salvation is not through law-keeping; it's through grace.

When a person becomes a Christian, our identity changes, giving us new ability to overcome our old barriers of exclusivity. For example, if you get your self-worth from being a hardworking person, you likely look down on people you consider lazy. If you get your self-worth from being an emotionally intuitive person, you probably don't like rationalistic people, who may seem cold to you; and if you get your self-worth from being a rational, reasonable person, you may brush off the concerns of the emotionally intuitive. In other words, if you accomplish your own salvation, if your self-image is based on something you achieve, you will tend to look down at other cultures, other classes, other vocational groups, other kinds of people, and other temperaments.

But the gospel doesn't start with strength or accomplishing your own salvation; it starts with weakness. It says God gives you a true salvation you can only receive when you humble yourself and admit your need. Christianity is not for the strong; it's for the people who know they're not. It's for those who admit they're weak, and then receive it by grace and are affirmed to the skies and valued by God's love. You can't feel superior to anybody—and that's what breaks through cultural barriers.

The key to it all is this: at the heart of the Bible is Jesus—God become man. The Spirit didn't just bring Philip to this meeting. The Spirit also directed this Ethiopian politician to the text, which is perhaps the heart of the whole Bible, because it is about substitutionary sacrifice.

Everything in the Bible points to how our salvation is not something we accomplish, and how Jesus Christ took our place, as our substitute, and did what was required to save us. The Bible sometimes talks about what Jesus did in the language of the battlefield. He fought the powers of sin and death for us. Sometimes it's the language of the marketplace. He paid our debt. Sometimes it's the language of the temple. He gave the ultimate sacrifice so we can be cleansed and acceptable in God's sight. Sometimes it's the language of the law court. He stood in our place and took our judgment and paid our penalty. And running through every single one of all of those different vocabularies is substitution.

The most compelling, most life-changing, most wonderful kind of story is one about someone dying to save other people. Years ago, when the last Harry Potter novel was about to come out and everyone was wondering how in the world J.K. Rowling would bring it all to a conclusion, I always knew (though nobody believed me!). I knew Harry had to die for his friends in order to save them. Why? Because there is no more compelling, wonderful, transforming storyline. If you know somebody has done it for you, nothing changes you more than that.

Some of you may know my favorite story from Charles Dickens is *A Tale of Two Cities*. At the famous conclusion, Sydney Carton breaks into the dungeon where his rival—who looks like him—is about to be guillotined. Carton smuggles this man, Charles Darnay, out of the prison and takes his place. He substitutes himself for the condemned man.[2] (The 1935 film starring Ronald Colman brings out the Christian themes beautifully.) There are other prisoners around, including a young seamstress waiting to be executed, too. She sees the man she thought was Darnay, looks at him, and realizes he's someone else. She asks him, "Are you dying for him?" He replies, "And his wife and child." In the 1935 film, she says something akin to, "Stranger, I don't think I can face my own death, but maybe if I hold the hand of someone as brave as you, I'll be able to do it." He agrees, and they go to the guillotine together.[3] She was transformed and strengthened by his substitutionary sacrifice, and it wasn't even for her.

How much more will you become an agent for the spread of the gospel, for a life of sacrifice, for giving yourself up so that others may live? How much more transformed will you be if you grasp God's substitutionary sacrifice for you and base your life on it?

CHAPTER

A PRAYER FOR GOD'S GUIDANCE

A PRAYER FOR GOD'S GUIDANCE

Father, thank you for sending Jesus to make the ultimate sacrifice for us. As we seek to build your church as Christians did in the book of Acts, we ask that you guide us toward encounters like Philip and the Ethiopian. Help us to display the radical inclusivity and exclusivity of your story in a compelling and life-changing way to those around us. Rather than ignoring those of different races, temperaments, economic statuses, or cultures, help us live as loving witnesses to them until we are invited in to share the good news of the gospel and delight in the common ground it holds for all of us. We pray this in your holy name, amen.

ENDNOTES

CHAPTER 2: INTRODUCTION

1. George Herbert, "Sin (I)," Poetry Foundation, accessed August 2, 2024, https://www.poetryfoundation.org/poems/44373/sin-i.

CHAPTER 3: THE INCLUSIVITY OF CHRISTIANITY

1. Lamin Sanneh, *Whose Religion is Christianity?* (Eerdmans, 2003).
2. These are average figures from Pew Research Center, "Global Christianity: A Report on the Size and Distribution of the World's Christian Population," December 19, 2011, www.pewforum.org/2011/12/19/global-christianity-exec/; Center for the Global Christianity; for more detailed statistics on the world Christian population, see resources at gordonconwell.edu/resources/csgc-resources.cfm; and Todd M. Johnson et al., *The World's Religions in Figures: An Introduction to International Religious Demography* (Oxford, UK: Wiley-Blackwell, 2013).
3. Sanneh, p. 15.
4. Richard Bauckham, *Bible and Mission: Christian Mission in a Postmodern World* (Grand Rapids, MI: Baker, 2003), p. 9. Bauckham's call for a "non-modern metanarrative" (pp. 83-89) is also relevant to our discussion. Bauckham's point is that without a "metanarrative" of some kind, you slide into soft relativism and individualism and this paves the way for oppression and inequality. But a "modern"

metanarrative, in Bauckham's analysis, is one used to oppress others. He argues that the Gospel of Jesus Christ provides a nonoppressive absolute truth, one that provides a norm outside of ourselves as the way to escape relativism and selfish individualism, yet one that cannot be used to oppress others, because at its heart it has a man dying for his enemies to forgive them.

5. Sanneh, p. 43.

CHAPTER 5: THE REASON FOR BOTH

1. Please note that this quotation is from the NIV 1984 translation, which differs from the NIV 2011 translation that readers may be more familiar with.
2. Charles Dickens, *A Tale of Two Cities* (Simon & Schuster, 2004).
3. Jack Conway and Robert Z. Leonard, *A Tale of Two Cities* (1935; United States: Metro-Goldwyn-Mayer (MGM)), film.

ABOUT

Gospel in Life

When Tim and Kathy Keller first started Redeemer Presbyterian Church of New York City in 1989, one of the first things a member of the congregation did was to start the sermon ministry, which recorded Sunday sermons and passed out cassette copies to anyone who wanted them.

This ministry grew exponentially, adding employees, equipment, and office space, and by the late '90s it was fulfilling paid subscriptions to people all over the world by mailing out thousands of sermon cassettes a year.

As people heard about Redeemer and Tim Keller, the "sermon ministry" continued to grow, eventually transitioning to a website where sermons and resources were sold digitally. In 2016 the sermon ministry of Redeemer church officially became known as Gospel in Life and began to expand the ways people could access the teaching and writing of Dr. Keller.

Today Gospel in Life presents the gospel-centered teaching and writing of Dr. Timothy J. Keller around the world. The sermons and talks available through Gospel in Life were preached by Dr. Keller from 1989 to 2017 while he was Senior Pastor at Redeemer Presbyterian Church. Through his sermons, books, articles, and resources, Gospel in Life seeks to bring about gospel transformation and to encourage Christians everywhere to live more missionally.

Gospel in Life now offers Dr. Keller's sermons through a podcast (downloaded millions of times each month), a radio broadcast on dozens of stations across the U.S., and an XM satellite radio broadcast that reaches all of North America. Additionally, Gospel in Life provides gospel-centered resources like seasonal devotionals, our quarterly journal, and the video series *Discovering the Gospel in Every Book of the Bible*. In 2023, through the faithful and generous gifts of Gospel in Life donors, Tim and Kathy were very pleased to see all of Dr. Keller's sermons become available for free on the Gospel in Life website.

At the beginning of 2023, Gospel in Life moved from being part of Redeemer Presbyterian Church and officially became part of Redeemer City to City—a ministry co-founded by Dr. Keller that supports gospel movements all over the world by training leaders and pastors and by helping them plant new churches in the global cities where they live.

We believe God is using our gospel-centered resources to transform lives and encourage Christians to live out their faith more fully in their neighborhoods, workplaces, and relationships. The name Gospel in Life reflects our conviction that the gospel truly changes everything in life.

Timothy Keller

As a family, the Kellers planted Redeemer Presbyterian Church in New York City in 1989, which grew to a weekly attendance of over 5,000 people, and through which God brought many other fruitful ministries, such as Redeemer City to City, the Center for Faith & Work, Hope for New York, and Redeemer Counseling Services, among others. After stepping down as Senior Pastor of Redeemer in July of 2017, Tim continued to serve at Redeemer City to City full-time, a ministry that has helped start more than 1,000 churches in over 150 cities, and trained or reached more than 79,000 leaders.

Tim was ordained into the Presbyterian Church in America in 1975 and served as pastor of West Hopewell Presbyterian Church from 1975 to 1984 and as senior pastor of Redeemer Presbyterian Church in New York City from 1989 to 2017.

Tim authored numerous books, with some of the best known being *The Reason for God*, *The Prodigal God*, and *The Meaning of Marriage*, which he co-authored with Kathy. Overall, he wrote 31 books that have sold over 6 million copies and have been translated into 29 languages.

Tim is survived by his wife, Kathy, who continues to minister through Gospel in Life and is working with her family to develop numerous unpublished works from Dr. Keller that they hope to publish in the coming years.

Christianity Today has said, "Fifty years from now, if evangelical Christians are widely known for their love of cities, their commitment to mercy and justice, and their love of their neighbors, Tim Keller will be remembered as a pioneer of the new urban Christians." For more info about Dr. Keller, visit **TimothyKeller.com**.

Redeemer City to City

Redeemer City to City supports pastors and leaders in church planting and contextualized urban ministry across the world. They also develop resources for their network in the form of books, group study materials, digital content, and online community—for leaders who seek to bring the power of the Christian gospel to every part of life. To learn more about their work, visit **RedeemerCitytoCity.com**.

Redeemer Presbyterian Church of NYC

The Redeemer congregation started with a few dozen people in 1989. It now draws over five thousand weekly attendees who meet in five Manhattan locations. Redeemer has birthed several ministries, including Hope for New York, the Center for Faith & Work, Redeemer Counseling Services, and Redeemer City to City. For more information, visit **Redeemer.com**.

Gospel in Life Podcasts

Tim Keller Sermons Podcast by Gospel in Life

Listen to sermons every Monday, Wednesday, and Friday by Tim Keller, founder of Redeemer Presbyterian Church in NYC and *New York Times* best-selling author of *The Reason for God: Belief in an Age of Skepticism*.

Listen at podcast.gospelinlife.com

Questioning Christianity with Tim Keller

A seven-part podcast series for people who are interested in exploring Christianity. This series will help listeners work through tough questions like: Can there be moral absolutes? Does life have meaning beyond what I make of it? Can hope exist in the face of death? Each of the talks and Q&A sessions were given by Tim Keller in 2019 before a live gathering in NYC, made up primarily of attendees who did not identify as Christian.

Listen at qcpodcast.gospelinlife.com

Cultivating a Healthy Marriage with Tim Keller

A short podcast series featuring the messages from the most popular sermon series of Dr. Tim Keller's time at Redeemer Presbyterian Church. Preached in 1991, this series was the basis for the bestselling book by Tim and Kathy Keller, *The Meaning of Marriage*. Whether you're single, married, widowed, or divorced, through this podcast you'll learn new ways to apply God's wisdom about marriage to your life.

Listen at marriage.gospelinlife.com

All Gospel in Life podcasts can be found by searching for **Gospel in Life** or **Tim Keller** wherever you listen to podcasts. You can also visit **gospelinlife.com/our-podcasts** to listen directly.

Visit our website to find a full catalog of Dr. Keller's sermons, talks, papers, and Bible studies at: **gospelinlife.com**

Read articles by Dr. Keller and people sharing about how the gospel has changed their life in the *Life in the Gospel* quarterly journal at: **gospelinlife.com/quarterly**

Subscribe to the Gospel in Life Youtube channel and watch video series by Dr. Keller like *Trusting God in Difficult Times* and *Discovering the Gospel in Every Book of the Bible*.

Follow Gospel in Life on Facebook, Instagram, X, and Threads